I0426192

Evaluation of the Sensitivity of Inventory and Monitoring National Parks to Nutrient Enrichment Effects from Atmospheric Nitrogen Deposition

Southeast Alaska Network (SEAN)

Natural Resource Report NPS/NRPC/ARD/NRR—2011/328

T. J. Sullivan
T. C. McDonnell
G. T. McPherson
S. D. Mackey
D. Moore

E&S Environmental Chemistry, Inc.
P.O. Box 609
Corvallis, OR 97339

February 2011

U.S. Department of the Interior
National Park Service
Natural Resource Program Center
Denver, Colorado

The National Park Service, Natural Resource Program Center publishes a range of reports that address natural resource topics of interest and applicability to a broad audience in the National Park Service and others in natural resource management, including scientists, conservation and environmental constituencies, and the public.

The Natural Resource Report Series is used to disseminate high-priority, current natural resource management information with managerial application. The series targets a general, diverse audience, and may contain NPS policy considerations or address sensitive issues of management applicability.

All manuscripts in the series receive the appropriate level of peer review to ensure that the information is scientifically credible, technically accurate, appropriately written for the intended audience, and designed and published in a professional manner.

This report received peer review by subject-matter experts who were not directly involved in the collection, analysis, or reporting of the data. Data in this report were collected and analyzed using methods based on established, peer-reviewed protocols and were analyzed and interpreted within the guidelines of the protocols.

Views, statements, findings, conclusions, recommendations, and data in this report do not necessarily reflect views and policies of the National Park Service, U.S. Department of the Interior. Mention of trade names or commercial products does not constitute endorsement or recommendation for use by the U.S. Government.

This report is available from Air Resources Division of the NPS (http://www.nature.nps.gov/air/Permits/ARIS/networks/n-sensitivity.cfm) and the Natural Resource Publications Management website (http://www.nature.nps.gov/publications/nrpm/).

Please cite this publication as:

Sullivan, T. J., T. C. McDonnell, G. T. McPherson, S. D. Mackey, and D. Moore. 2011. Evaluation of the sensitivity of inventory and monitoring national parks to nutrient enrichment effects from atmospheric nitrogen deposition: Southeast Alaska Network (SEAN). Natural Resource Report NPS/NRPC/ARD/NRR—2011/328. National Park Service, Denver, Colorado.

NPS 953/106692, February 2011

Southeast Alaska Network (SEAN)

National maps of atmospheric N emissions and deposition are provided in Maps A and B as context for subsequent network data presentations. Map A shows county level emissions of total N for the year 2002. Map B shows total N deposition, again for the year 2002. Regional deposition data are not available for Alaska, but N deposition would be expected to be very low throughout most, but not necessarily all, of Alaska. There are five active NADP/NTN wet deposition monitoring sites in Alaska: Poker Creek, Juneau, Denali National Park, Gates of the Arctic National Park, and Katmai National Park, with data collected since 1980 at Denali and since 1993 at Poker Creek. The other three monitoring sites have been added within the last decade. There are also CASTNET dry deposition measurements at DENA and Poker Flats. At all monitored sites in Alaska, wet N deposition has consistently been less than 1 kg N/ha/yr, and it has been less than 0.5 kg N/ha/yr at all monitored sites except Juneau. The dry N deposition measurements by CASTNET have also been low, below about 0.25 kg N/ha/yr for each site and year measured. Thus, the sparse available atmospheric N deposition data for Alaska are consistent with the general understanding that atmospheric deposition tends to be very low at national park lands within Alaska. It can be assumed that N deposition in each of the Alaskan networks would be lower than 1 to 2 kg/ha/yr, on average, across each of those networks.

There are three park units in the Southeast Alaska Network: Glacier Bay (GLBA), Klondike Gold Rush (KLGO), and Sitka (SITK). Only GLBA is larger than 100 square miles.

Total annual N emissions, by county, are shown in Map C for lands in and surrounding the Southeast Alaska Network. County-level emissions within the network are uniformly less than 1 ton per square mile. Map D is not shown because there are no point source emissions of oxidized (nitrogen oxides, NO_x) or reduced (ammonia, NH_3) N in this network. Urban centers within the network and within a 300 mile buffer around the network are shown in Map E. There are no urban centers larger than 50,000 people, and only one urban center larger than 25,000 people.

Map F is not shown because there are no regional N deposition data available. Based on the near total absence of population centers and lack of point sources, we expect total N deposition throughout this network to be less than 1 to 2 kg N/ha/yr.

Land cover in and around the network is shown in Map G. The predominant cover types within this network are generally forested and perennial ice and snow.

Map H shows the distribution within the parks that occur in this network of the five vegetation types thought to be most responsive to nutrient N enrichment effects (arctic herbaceous, alpine, grassland and meadow, wetland, and arid and semi-arid). The only park of any magnitude is GLBA. The predominant sensitive vegetation types in this park are alpine and wetland vegetation.

Park lands requiring special protection against potential adverse impacts associated with nutrient N enrichment from atmospheric N deposition are shown in Map I. Also shown on Map I are all federal lands designated as wilderness, both lands managed by NPS and also lands managed by other federal agencies. The land designations used to identify this heightened protection included

Class I designation under the CAAA and wilderness designation. There are no Class I areas within this network, but a large percentage of the overall network area is designated wilderness.

Network rankings are given in Figures A through C as the average ranking of the Pollutant Exposure, Ecosystem Sensitivity, and Park Protection metrics, respectively. Figure D shows the overall network Summary Risk ranking. In each figure, the rank for this particular network is highlighted to show its relative position compared with the ranks of the other 31 networks.

The Southeast Alaska Network ranks in the lowest quintile, among networks, in N Pollutant Exposure (Figure A). Nitrogen emissions and expected N deposition within the network are both very low. The network Ecosystem Sensitivity ranking is also very low, within the lowest quintile among networks (Figure B). This is because there is limited vegetation in the I&M parks that occur in this network that includes vegetation types expected to be especially sensitive to nutrient enrichment effects from N deposition, and there are no high-elevation lakes. This network ranks in the top quintile in Park Protection, having substantial amounts of protected lands (Figure C).

In combination, the network rankings for Pollutant Exposure, Ecosystem Sensitivity, and Park Protection yield an overall Network Risk ranking that is in the lowest quintile among all networks (Figure D). The overall level of concern for nutrient N enrichment effects on I&M parks within this network is considered Very Low.

Similarly, park rankings are given in Figures E through H for the same metrics. In the case of the park rankings, we only show in the figures the parks that are larger than 100 square miles. Relative ranks for all parks, including the smaller parks, are given in Table A and Appendix B. As for the network ranking figures, the park ranking figures highlight those parks that occur in this network to show their relative position compared with parks in the other 31 networks. Note that the rankings shown in Figures E through H reflect the rank of a given park compared with all other parks, irrespective of size.

All three parks in this network rank in the lowest quintile for Pollutant Exposure (Figure E, Table A). Ecosystem Sensitivity is ranked in the second lowest quintile for GLBA but somewhat higher for the two smaller parks (Figure F, Table A). GLBA is in the highest quintile in Park Protection (Figure G), whereas the other two parks are in the middle quintile for this theme (Table A).

The combined Summary Park Risk ranking places GLBA in the second lowest quintile among parks (Figure H). Thus, this park appears to have a Low risk of nutrient N enrichment effects. The risk for the other two parks is considered Very Low (Table A).

Table A. Relative rankings of individual I&M parks within the network for Pollutant Exposure, Ecosystem Sensitivity, Park Protection, and Summary Risk from atmospheric nutrient N enrichment.

I&M Parks[2] in Network	Relative Ranking of Individual Parks[1]			
	Pollutant Exposure	Ecosystem Sensitivity	Park Protection	Summary Risk
Glacier Bay	Very Low	Low	Very High	Low
Klondike Gold Rush	Very Low	High	Moderate	Very Low
Sitka	Very Low	Moderate	Moderate	Very Low

[1] Relative park rankings are designated according to quintile ranking, among all I&M Parks, from the lowest quintile (very low risk) to the highest quintile (very high risk).

[2] Park name is printed in bold italic for parks larger than 100 square miles.

Map A.   National map of total N emissions by county for the year 2002. Both oxidized (nitrogen oxides, NO_x) and reduced (ammonia, NH_3) forms of N are included. The total is expressed in tons per square mile per year. (Source of data: EPA National Emissions Inventory, http://www.epa.gov/ttn/chief/net/2002inventory.html)

Map B.   Regional deposition data are not available for Alaska. Total N deposition throughout most areas in Alaska is expected to be low, below about 2 kilograms of N per hectare per year. Total N deposition for the continental United States is presented for context here for the year 2002, expressed in units of kilograms of N deposited from the atmosphere to the earth surface per hectare per year. Wet and dry forms of both oxidized (nitrogen oxides, NO_x) and reduced (ammonia, NH_3) N are included. For the eastern half of the country, wet deposition values were derived from interpolated measured values from NADP (three-year average centered on 2002) and dry deposition values were derived from 12-km CMAQ model projections for 2002. For the western half of the country, both wet and dry deposition values were derived from 36-km CMAQ model projections for 2002. NADP interpolations were performed using the approach of Grimm and Lynch (1997). CMAQ model projections were provided by Robin Dennis, U.S. EPA.

Map C.   Total N emissions by county for lands surrounding the network, expressed as tons of N emitted into the atmosphere per square mile per year. The total includes both oxidized (nitrogen oxides, NO_x) and reduced (ammonia, NH_3) N. (Source of data: EPA National Emissions Inventory, http://www.epa.gov/ttn/chief/net/2002inventory.html)

Map E.   Urban centers having more than 10,000 people within the network and within a 300-mile buffer around the perimeter of the network. (Source of data: U.S. Census 2000)

Map G.   Land cover types in and around the network, based on the National Land Cover dataset. (Source of data: National Land Cover Dataset, http://www.mrlc.gov/nlcd_multizone_map.php)

Total Nitrogen Emissions by County
United States
(tons per square mile per year)

Puerto Rico

Hawaii

Alaska

Total Nitrogen Emissions
tons per sq. mi per year

Less than 1
Greater than 1 and up to 5
Greater than 5 and up to 20
Greater than 20 and up to 50
Greater than 50 and up to 100
Greater than 100 and up to 618

NPS Networks
I & M Parks

Data Source: National Emissions Inventory (EPA, 2002)
Projection: World Mercator, WGS 1984
Produced for: National Park Service, Air Resources Division, 2010
Prepared by: E&S Environmental Chemistry

Map A

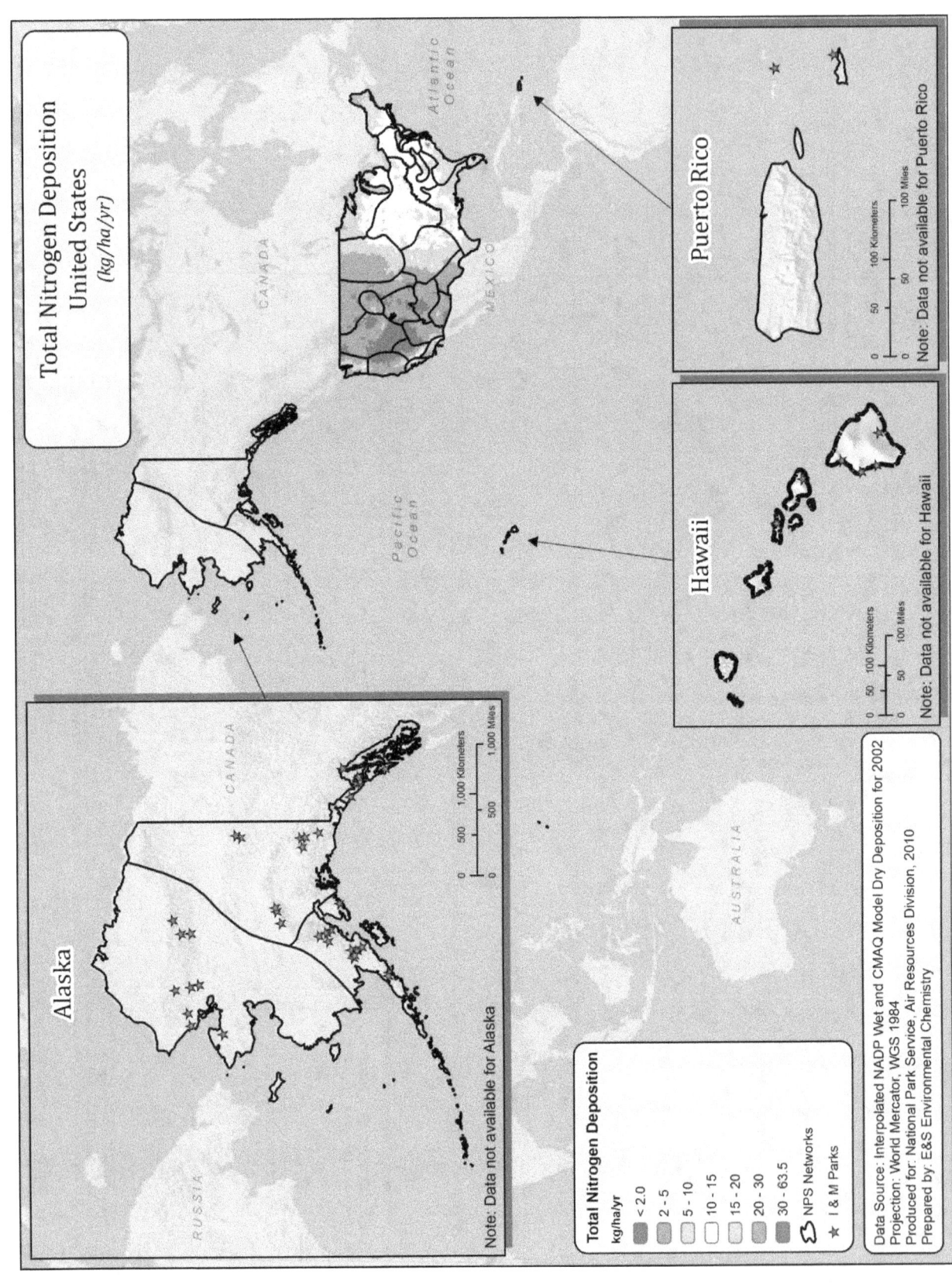

Total Nitrogen Deposition United States
(kg/ha/yr)

Total Nitrogen Deposition

kg/ha/yr
- < 2.0
- 2 - 5
- 5 - 10
- 10 - 15
- 15 - 20
- 20 - 30
- 30 - 63.5

NPS Networks

★ I & M Parks

Puerto Rico

Note: Data not available for Puerto Rico

Hawaii

Note: Data not available for Hawaii

Alaska

Note: Data not available for Alaska

Data Source: Interpolated NADP Wet and CMAQ Model Dry Deposition for 2002
Projection: World Mercator, WGS 1984
Produced for: National Park Service, Air Resources Division, 2010
Prepared by: E&S Environmental Chemistry

Map B

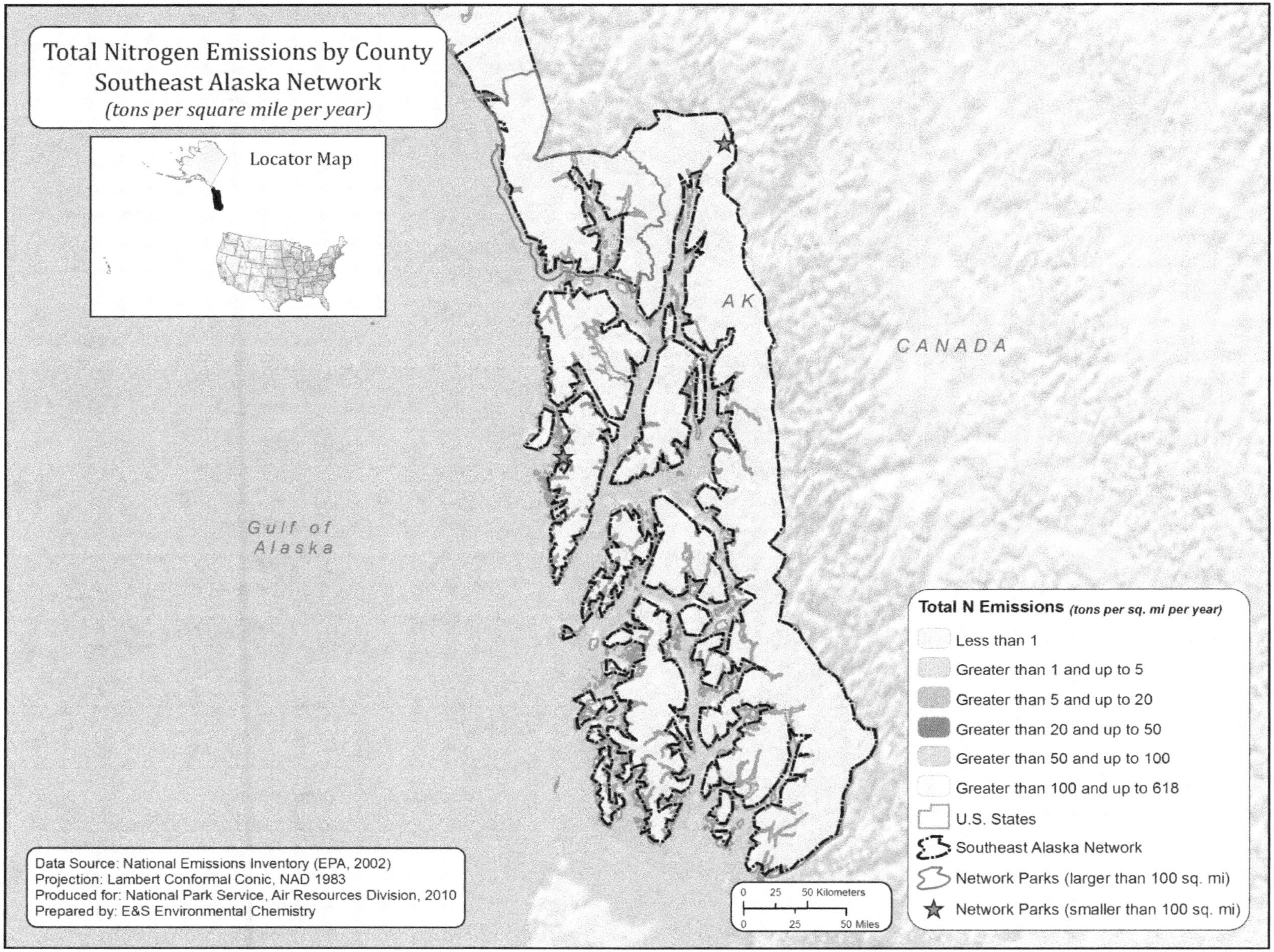

Total Nitrogen Emissions by County
Southeast Alaska Network
(tons per square mile per year)

Locator Map

CANADA

AK

Gulf of
Alaska

Total N Emissions *(tons per sq. mi per year)*

Less than 1
Greater than 1 and up to 5
Greater than 5 and up to 20
Greater than 20 and up to 50
Greater than 50 and up to 100
Greater than 100 and up to 618
U.S. States
Southeast Alaska Network
Network Parks (larger than 100 sq. mi)
Network Parks (smaller than 100 sq. mi)

25   50 Kilometers
0
0   25   50 Miles

Data Source: National Emissions Inventory (EPA, 2002)
Projection: Lambert Conformal Conic, NAD 1983
Produced for: National Park Service, Air Resources Division, 2010
Prepared by: E&S Environmental Chemistry

Map C

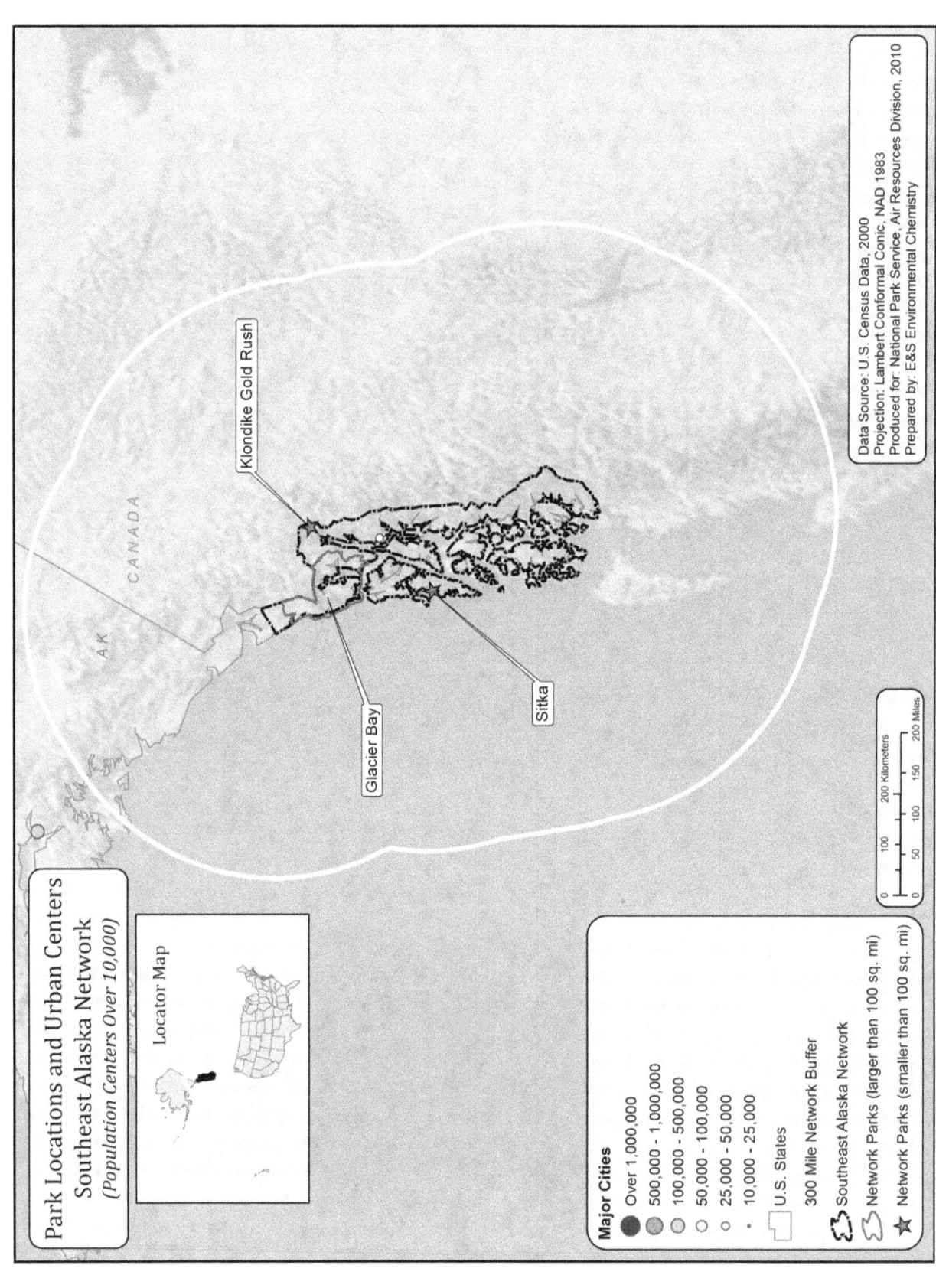

Park Locations and Urban Centers
Southeast Alaska Network
(Population Centers Over 10,000)

Locator Map

Major Cities
- Over 1,000,000
- 500,000 - 1,000,000
- 100,000 - 500,000
- 50,000 - 100,000
- 25,000 - 50,000
- 10,000 - 25,000

U.S. States

300 Mile Network Buffer

Southeast Alaska Network

Network Parks (larger than 100 sq. mi)

Network Parks (smaller than 100 sq. mi)

Klondike Gold Rush

Glacier Bay

Sitka

CANADA

A K

Data Source: U.S. Census Data, 2000
Projection: Lambert Conformal Conic, NAD 1983
Produced for: National Park Service, Air Resources Division, 2010
Prepared by: E&S Environmental Chemistry

0   50   100   200 Kilometers
0   50   100   150   200 Miles

Map E

SEAN-8

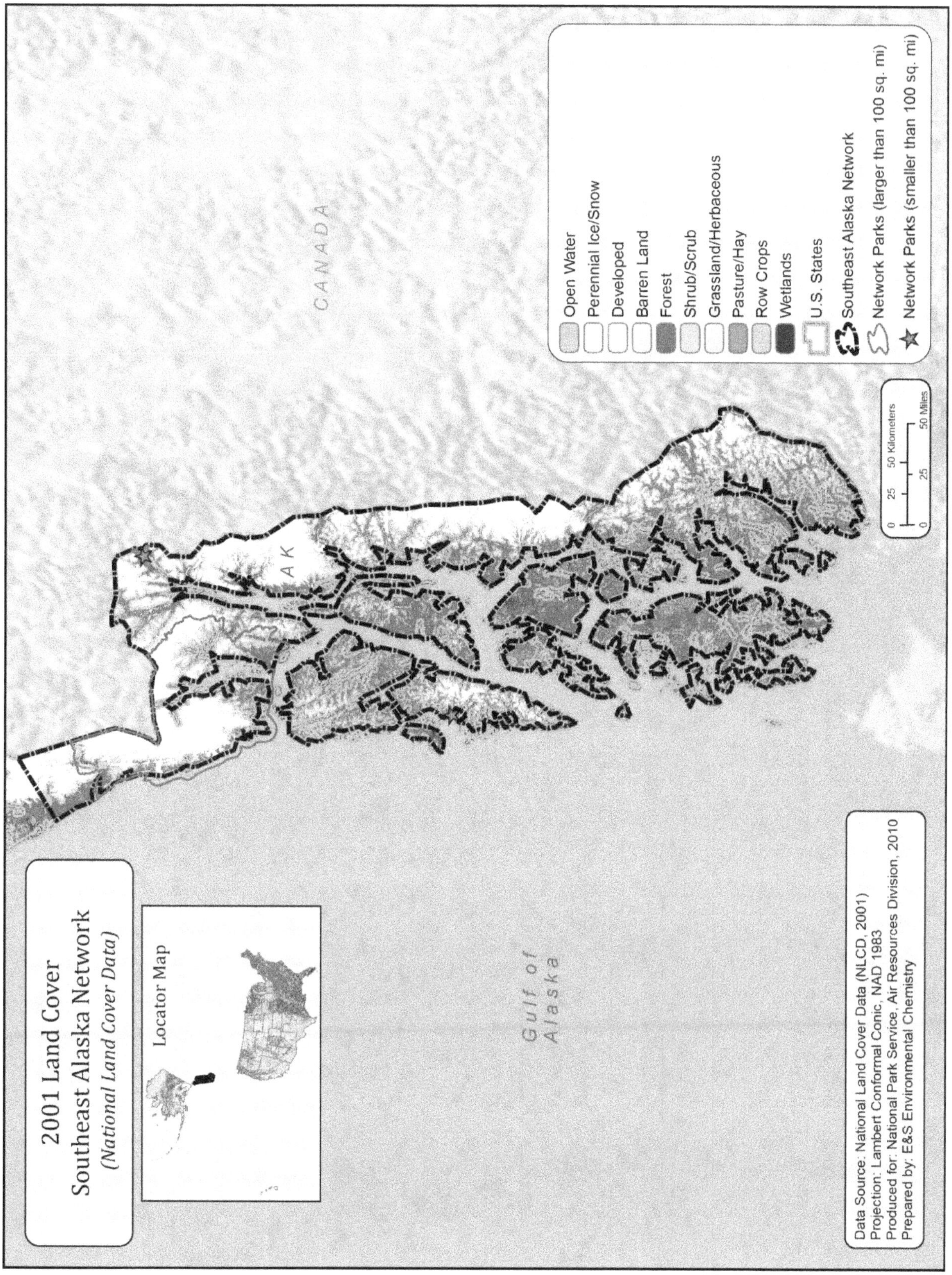

2001 Land Cover
Southeast Alaska Network
(National Land Cover Data)

Locator Map

Gulf of
Alaska

CANADA

AK

Open Water
Perennial Ice/Snow
Developed
Barren Land
Forest
Shrub/Scrub
Grassland/Herbaceous
Pasture/Hay
Row Crops
Wetlands
U.S. States
Southeast Alaska Network
Network Parks (larger than 100 sq. mi)
Network Parks (smaller than 100 sq. mi)

0   25   50 Kilometers
0   25   50 Miles

Data Source: National Land Cover Data (NLCD, 2001)
Projection: Lambert Conformal Conic, NAD 1983
Produced for: National Park Service, Air Resources Division, 2010
Prepared by: E&S Environmental Chemistry

Map G

SEAN-9

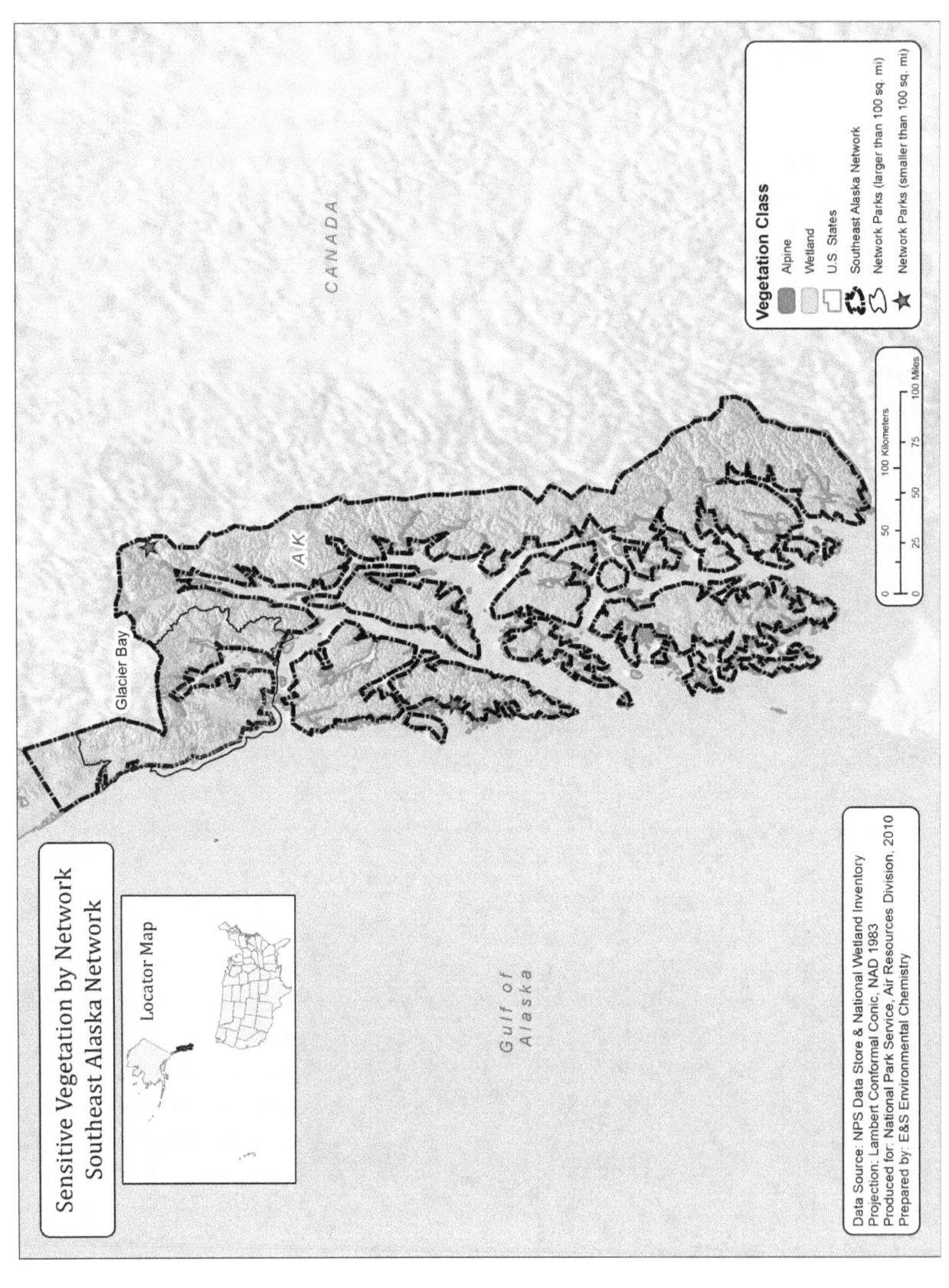

Sensitive Vegetation by Network
Southeast Alaska Network

Locator Map

Glacier Bay

A K

CANADA

Gulf of
Alaska

Vegetation Class

- Alpine
- Wetland
- U.S. States
- Southeast Alaska Network
- Network Parks (larger than 100 sq. mi)
- Network Parks (smaller than 100 sq. mi)

0   50   100 Kilometers
0   25   50   75   100 Miles

Data Source: NPS Data Store & National Wetland Inventory
Projection: Lambert Conformal Conic, NAD 1983
Produced for: National Park Service, Air Resources Division, 2010
Prepared by: E&S Environmental Chemistry

Map H

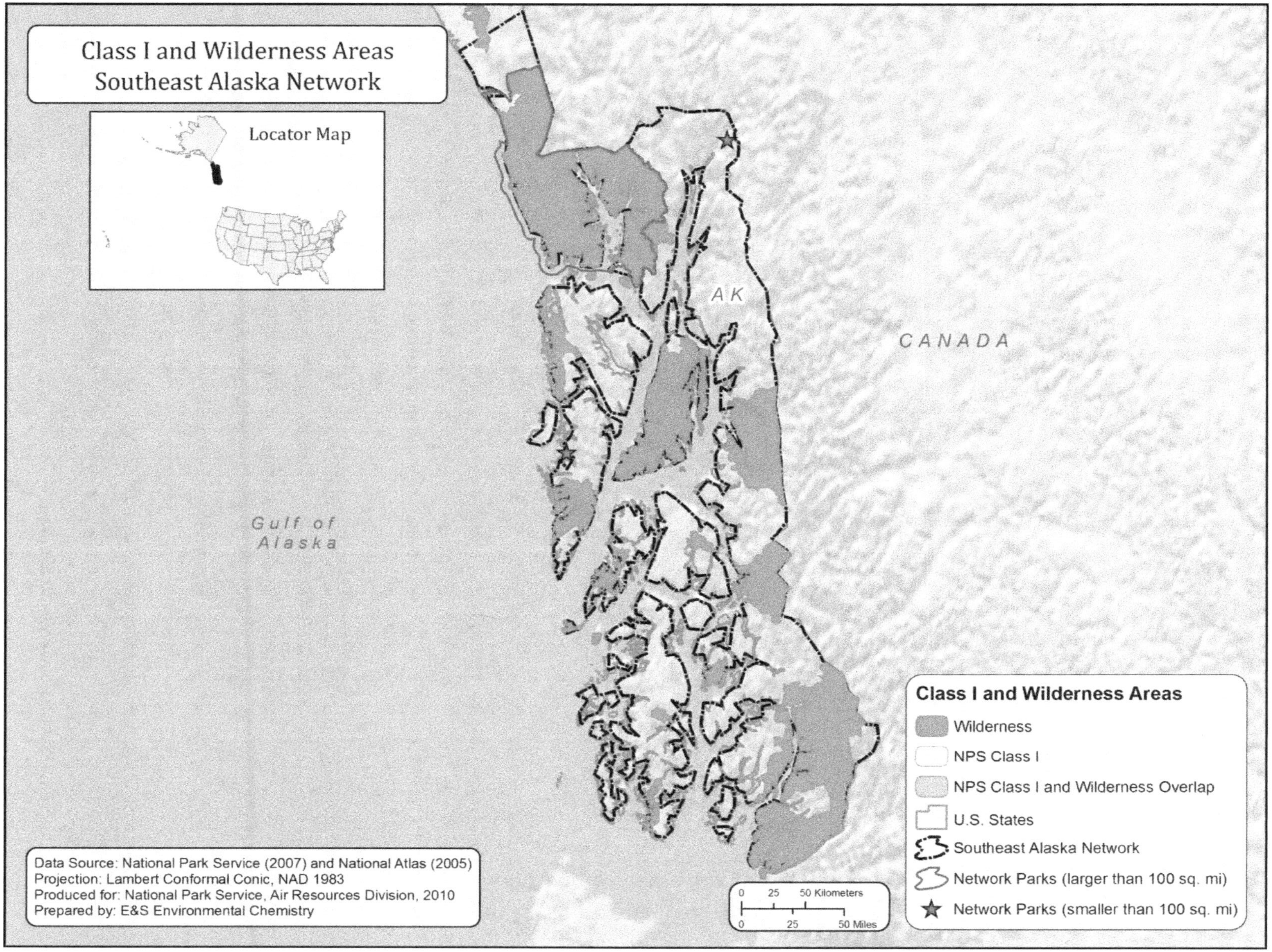

Class I and Wilderness Areas
Southeast Alaska Network

Locator Map

CANADA

AK

Gulf of Alaska

Class I and Wilderness Areas

- Wilderness
- NPS Class I
- NPS Class I and Wilderness Overlap
- U.S. States
- Southeast Alaska Network
- ☆ Network Parks (larger than 100 sq. mi)
- ☆ Network Parks (smaller than 100 sq. mi)

0   25   50 Kilometers
0   25   50 Miles

Data Source: National Park Service (2007) and National Atlas (2005)
Projection: Lambert Conformal Conic, NAD 1983
Produced for: National Park Service, Air Resources Division, 2010
Prepared by: E&S Environmental Chemistry

Map I

Figure A

Figure B

SEAN-13

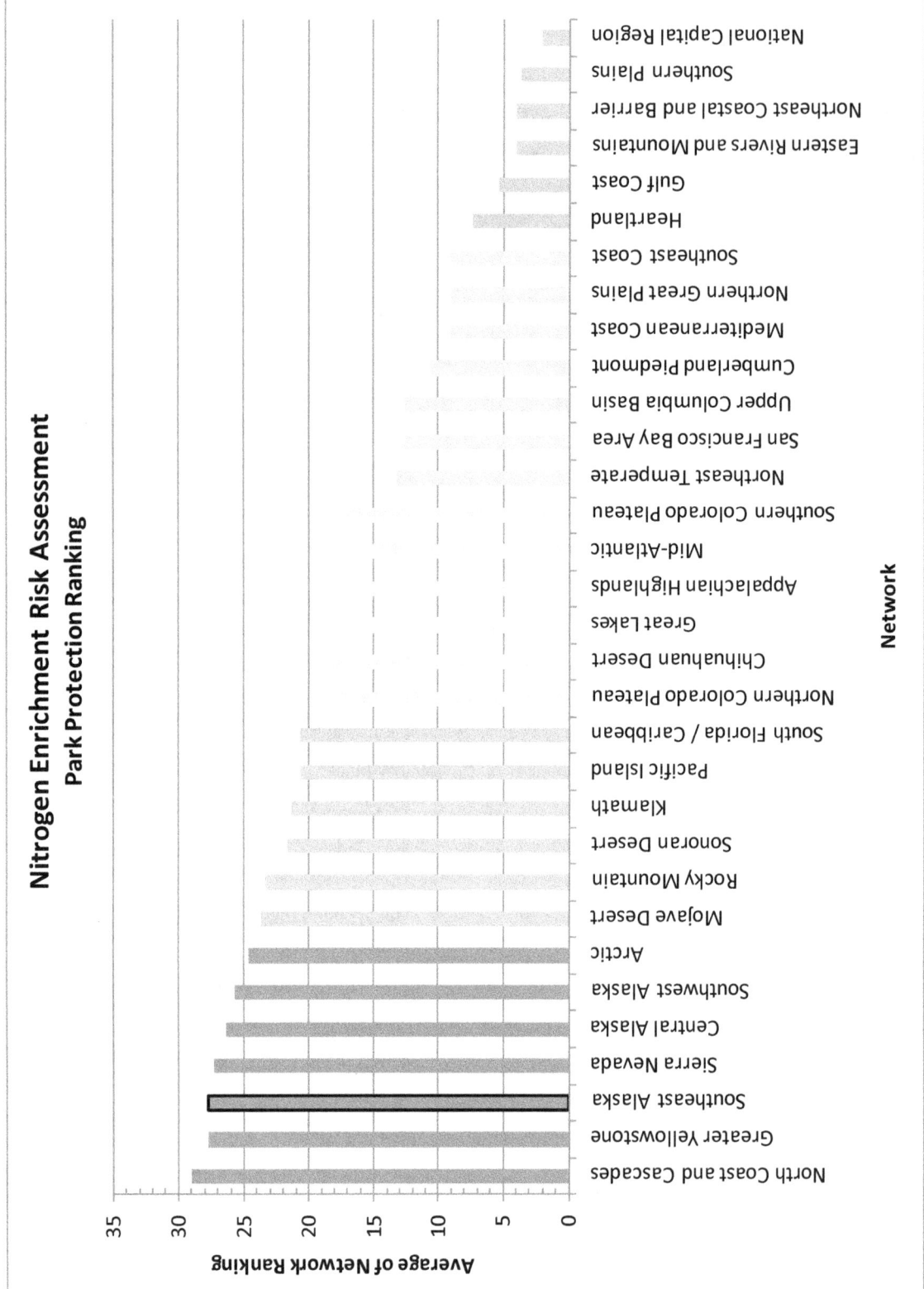

Figure C

Nitrogen Enrichment Risk Assessment
Summary Risk Ranking

Average of Network Ranking

Network

Sierra Nevada
North Coast and Cascades
South Florida / Caribbean
Greater Yellowstone
Mojave Desert
Great Lakes
Klamath
Rocky Mountain
Pacific Island
Northern Colorado Plateau
Sonoran Desert
San Francisco Bay Area
Appalachian Highlands
Mediterranean Coast
Mid-Atlantic
Southern Colorado Plateau
Southeast Coast
Northern Great Plains
Cumberland Piedmont
Northeast Coastal and Barrier
Chihuahuan Desert
Northeast Temperate
Heartland
Arctic
Southwest Alaska
Central Alaska
National Capital Region
Southeast Alaska
Gulf Coast
Southern Plains
Eastern Rivers and Mountains
Upper Columbia Basin

Figure D

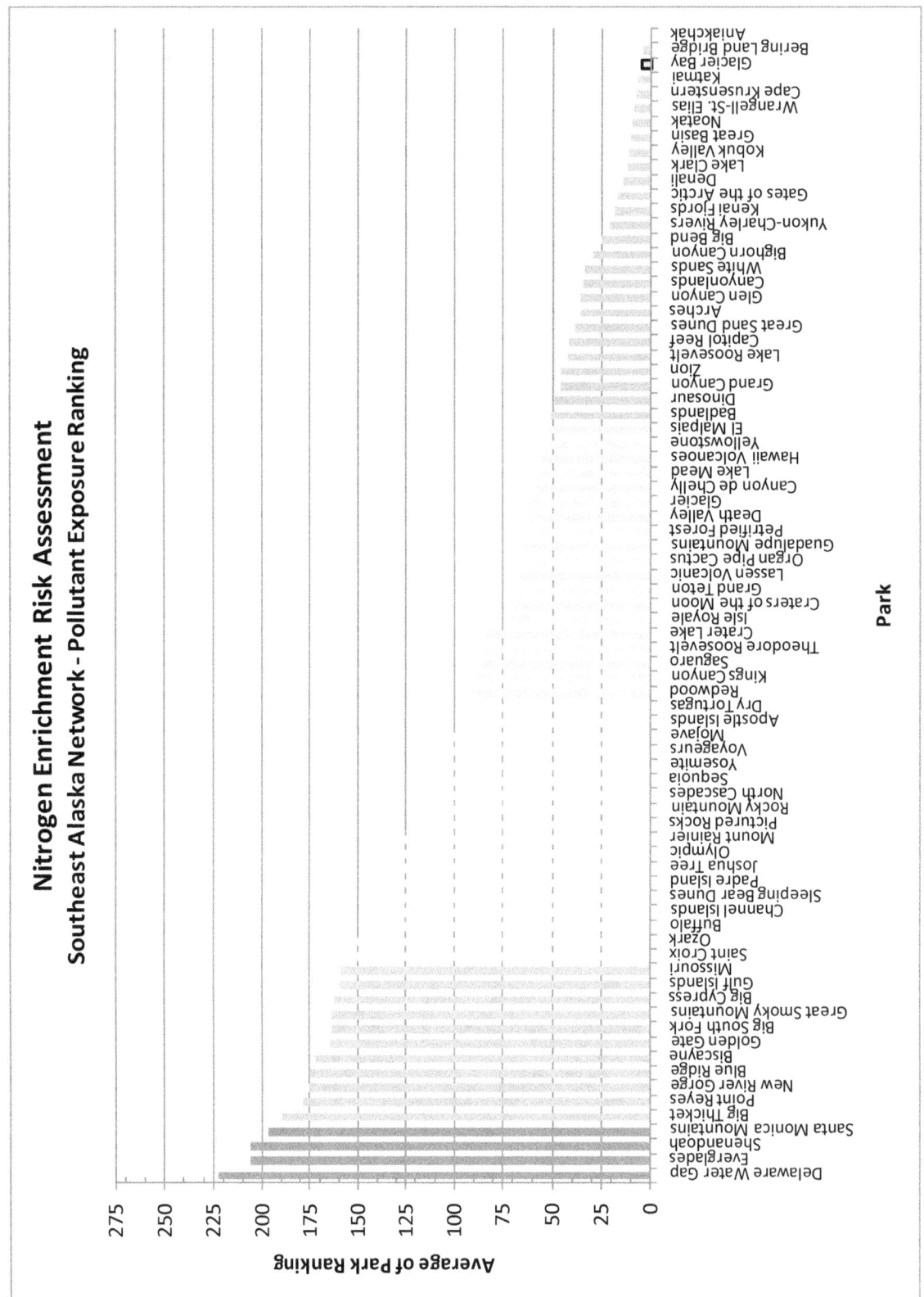

Figure E

SEAN-16

Figure F

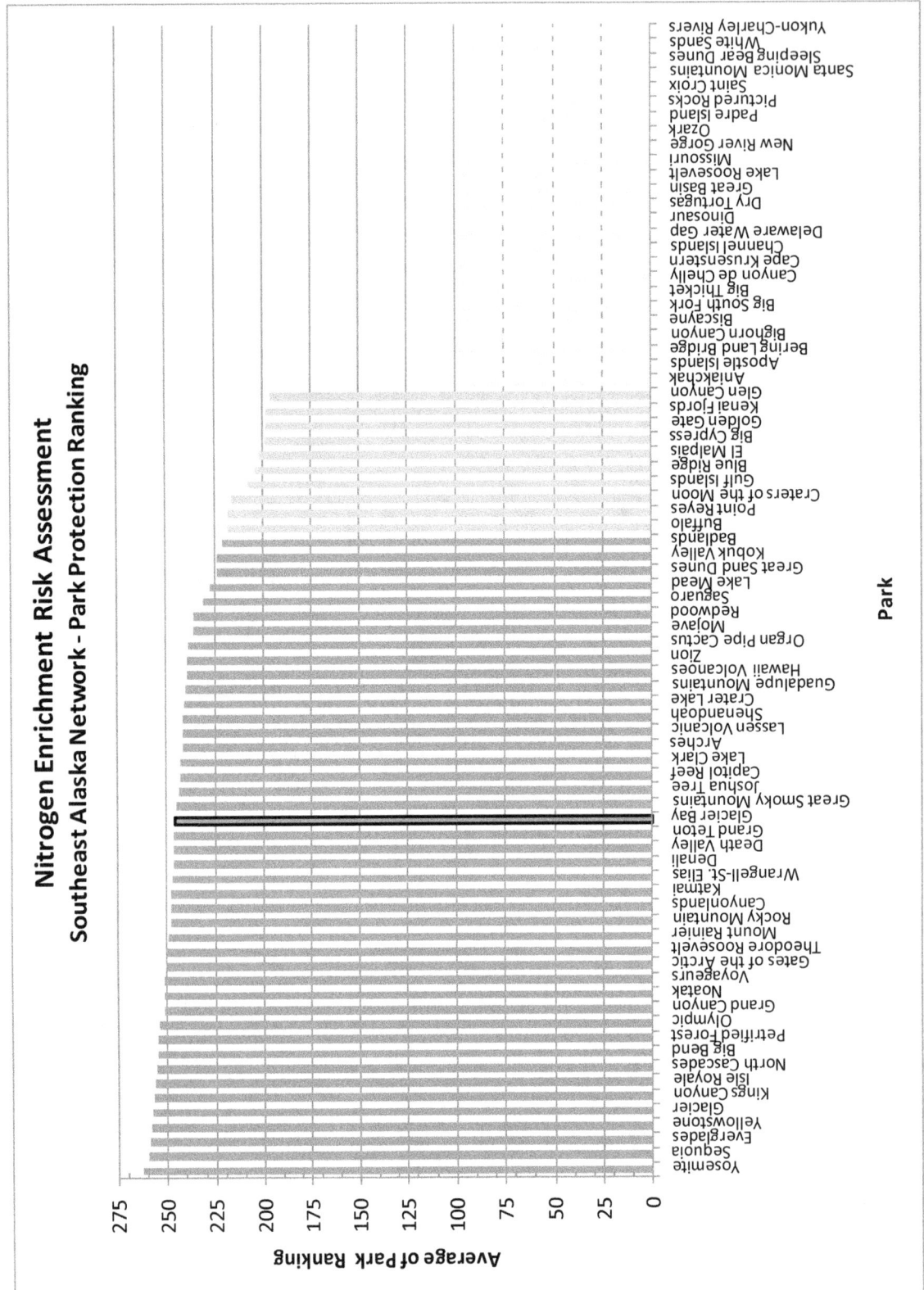

Figure G

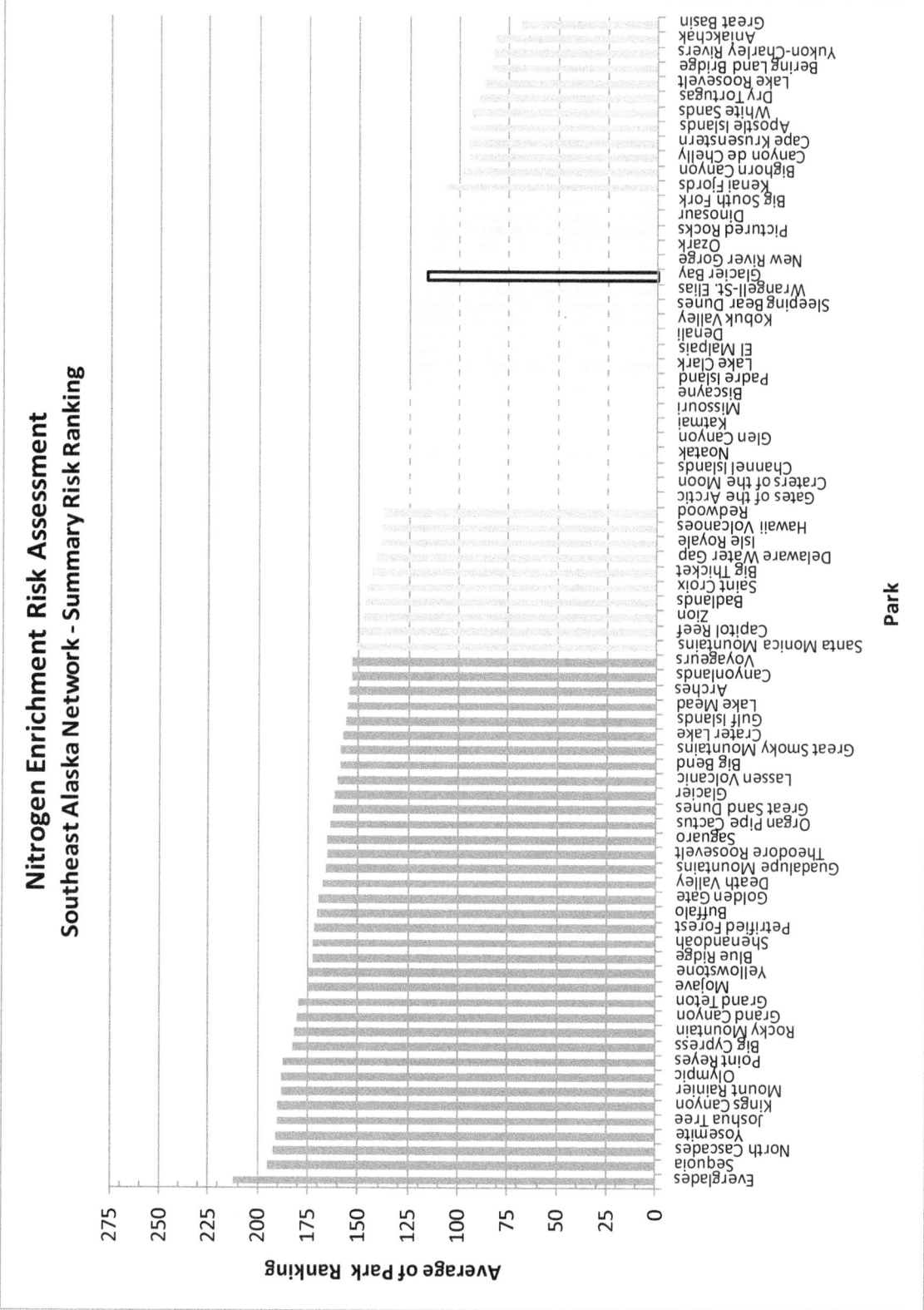

Nitrogen Enrichment Risk Assessment
Southeast Alaska Network - Summary Risk Ranking

Figure H

NPS 953/106692, February 2011

National Park Service
U.S. Department of the Interior

Natural Resource Program Center
Air Resources Division
PO Box 25287
Denver, CO 80225

www.nature.nps.gov/air

EXPERIENCE YOUR AMERICA ™